The Green Bookcase
2nd Edition

The Green Bookcase
2nd Edition

by William Heyen
with Photographs by Karla Linn Merrifield

Hollybrook House Press

No. 66

$8.0

Ontario Review

Poetry Alicia Ostriker, William Heyen, Joan Murray
Fiction Brad Morrow, Laurence de Looze, Juned Subhan
Drama Peter Maloney, "Leash" from Abu Ghraib Triptych
Graphics Gloria Vanderbilt, "The Dark is Light Enough"
with an Afterword by

In memory of Raymond J. Smith, 1930-2008

Foreword to the 2nd Edition:
Dream of Beauty

William Heyen has enriched the lives of readers of American poetry for well over fifty years. Indeed, Bill stands alongside such literary luminaries as Adelaide Crapsey and John Ashbery as one of the major figures in the history of Western New York poetry. And, like Ashbery, Bill's interest in the visual arts has long been apparent. He collaborated with California artist DeLoss McGraw in "A Painter's Response to Poetry," held at the Memorial Art Gallery in 2000. A year later Bill worked with renowned sculptor Wendell Castle on *Lord Dragonfly's Chair* now in the permanent collection of the Memorial Art Gallery.

There, several of Bill's poems from his book *Lord Dragonfly* were hand-carved into Wendell's cherry wood bench. And, over a decade later, Bill participated with other area artists (historic and contemporary) in the establishment of Poets Walk, an engaging, interactive installation flanking the Memorial Art Gallery. A year later in 2013, Bill collaborated with distinguished artists Robert Marx and Sue Leopard, creating two broadsides to commemorate the Gallery's Centennial.

The Green Bookcase attests to Bill's interest in the visual arts. That is, it seems a "readymade" or "found object" in the tradition of much 20th- and 21st-century sculpture. Though more monumental than surrealist sculptor Joseph Cornell's small glass boxes, Bill's bookcase also evinces memory, mystery and our human conception of time. Whether formally related to the readymade or installation art, Bill, the poet/artist, fully recognizes this affinity to the visual arts when describing the "rhythmic colors & textures & geometries" of the bookcase. As Bill once said to me, *The Green Bookcase* incontestably represents an "intersection of life & the fine arts."

An ancient Chinese proverb says, "a book is like a garden carried in your pocket." If true, what glorious landscapes are to be found within *The Green Bookcase*!

Grant Holcomb
Director Emeritus, Memorial Art Gallery/University of Rochester

I.

　　At the back of my garage here in the Village of
Brockport in western New York State is a small enclosed
shed/storage area. On the morning of May 15, 2007, I was
sitting beside the seven-foot wood bookcase where I keep
literary magazines that have published my writings over
the decades—the mags became too many to keep in the house,
& I've not had the heart to bequeath them to the recycle
container, & they are occasionally useful toward this or
that project, & they do have sentimental value—when light
streaked in from over my right shoulder to create an aura
that enveloped the whole rectangle. I had the sudden
intuition that case & contents had come to unity,
to Oneness, had come to be a work of art.

A *work* in that I keep making it, adding to it (as
do the editors, designers, artists, printers, binders
who create the magazines themselves). *Art* by way of this
object's harmonious intensifications of its own reason for
being; its rhythmic colors & textures & geometries; its
functionally informed complex of personal & communal memory;
its <u>beauty</u> as it invites viewing & may even seem to behold
the viewer as does Rilke's torso of Apollo. Art by way of
how it variously engages what might be art's supreme theme:
Time…. My dozen other bookcases are much more sure of
themselves, are less eccentric, do not have the depth
of character of this one….

Soon after my discovery, I wanted someone else to see this unique entity, walk up to it, sit in the rusted & paint-splotched metal chair (itself part of this ensemble) where its companion often sat—left shoulder toward the case, light coming from the right—& even handle/peruse one or more of the voluminous constituent artifacts themselves that he'd arranged, beginning with the top left shelf, chronologically. (In a university rare books archive, he'd seen the magazines in which he'd published arranged alphabetically by magazine title.) Some are so thin that they are hidden. (Imagine the aspirations of even the most ephemeral of these magazines.) He protected most in plastic bags, kept some shrink-wrapped as received. Often there are two copies—he kept no more than two—of the same issue of the same magazine—spondees of the brush in this painting, of notes in this musical composition.

Each magazine, the experiencer could be sure, whether the currently extant & prestigious The New Yorker or *Harper's* or *The Atlantic* or *The Southern Review* or *Kenyon Review* or *Virginia Quarterly Review* or *Chautauqua* or *Poetry* or *TriQuarterly*, or the now-defunct *Striver's Row* or *Scimitar and Song* or *The Galley Sail Review* or *Tuatara* or *Rapport* or *Longshot* or *Bluefish* or *American Weave* or *Approach* or *Toad Highway* or *The Husk* or *Motive* or *Trace* or *Jeopardy* or *Our Original Sins* or *Back Door* or *Fragments* or *Fireweed* or *Thistle* or *Desperate Act* or *Potato Eyes* or *The Windhorse Review* or *Crop Dust* or *The Page*

or *Triad* (a Texas quarterly that lasted only two issues) or a couple hundred others, gave pleasure & a sense of accomplishment when it arrived from however far. He had at least an illusion of being read. Many, especially earlier ones, moved with the writer from place to place, even across the Atlantic (*The Saturday Review* with a couple of his reviews that arrived when he taught in Germany in 1971-72) or the Pacific (*American Poetry Review* with his picture on the cover & a suite of poems that arrived when he taught at the University of Hawaii in 1985). Now, here, they & he are home, except for some that are missing—his own collection of his publications is not complete.

On top of the bookcase are three maroon file boxes that hold folded, tabloid-sized magazines, his least favorite format, but these are also part of this sculpture made of wood & words, glue & thread, artwork/story/essay/poetry. But *The Green Bookcase* is still a work-in-progress, too: there may be just about enough shelf-space left to hold the magazines that welcome him during what remains of his pre-posthumous existence. If not, he could add a few more file boxes. Or he could add an "Annex," as the greatest American democratic poet, Walt Whitman, added annexes to his *Leaves of Grass*.

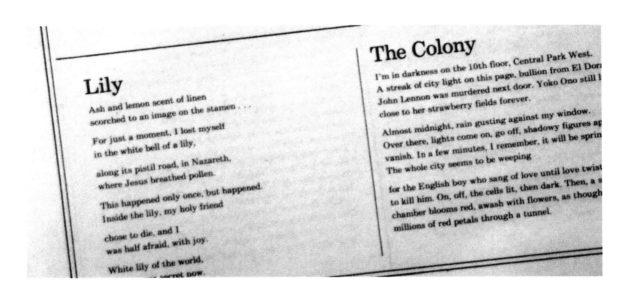

Maybe, though, William should revise, should ripsaw down to just one copy of each magazine—this would give him at least a third more space. But then *The Green Bookcase* wouldn't hum the same sounds, & the duplicate copies seem to satisfy his need to hoard—he's the son of parents who struggled through the Great Depression…. Maybe, for a good sense of old-fashioned artistic closure, he could just stop publishing in magazines as shelf-space closed in on him….

Back to the first person. On the bottom shelf I've kept a clock that Werner made. I hadn't thought about this before, but I'm moving toward him, toward his suspended time, his eternity, magazine by magazine, poem by poem. I've never bothered to replace its battery.

Also in the bookcase is a glass-sided walnut box that holds used pens of mine that I've been throwing into it for years. I feel somewhat guilty about these memorabilia/ realia, should probably switch to a different pen, but I've become so comfortable with this Japanese Energel .07 metal-tip model that I've stayed with it.

Here, in the green bookcase, the dead pens do not add
to the waste stream as they support & surround a large
topaz-colored glass turtle given to me by my wife, who found
it at a garage sale in about 1980 in her home village of
Forestville, west of Buffalo. This terrapin's carapace lifts
off. Inside, are several other turtles given to me by family
& friends…. The turtle: my often-dreamed totem animal. (If
you have time to take a look, see my poem "Annuli"—several
of its nineteen sections appear here in *Ontario Review*,
#68 [2007]). Let's say that this box is also a little
magazine. We'll call it *The Turtle Review*. If it ever ceases
publication, no other magazine will be able to take its
place. In fact, if it ever ceases publication, it will mean
that no one is doing any reading, that even god has ceased
to read us.

Ironic, isn't it: my books & broadsides & the hundreds of anthologies that have published me are inside my home in my study. But this bookcase's minor bibliographic "C" items had to keep hot every summer & cold every winter out in the shed. Now I know that when I've passed by it & ignored it, or sat by it or added to it so many times over the years, *The Green Bookcase*—its exoskeleton shaped by an anonymous maker I don't know how long ago—I like to think 1940, the year I was born—in muted but lyrical ways as an organic & growing form, & against the grain of our age of diminishing print culture, diminishing species, was witnessing/ describing/defining/imagining itself as a work of art. Like any work of what Ezra Pound called "first intensity," it was readying itself for what I might in time come to realize about it.

II.

Afterthoughts/shelf fillers ending with a story & a dream poem:

i.
I'm glad that *The Green Bookcase* has a back, a frame, that its shelves are not vulnerable from behind.

ii.
I'm glad its exoskeleton is a muted green, the paint original. & I'm glad that this one is painted—all my other bookcases are stained.

iii.

I'm glad that paragraphs fill the shelves of this prose piece, & that I can justify its right margin.

iv.

I'm glad the object is taller than I am (I'm 6'5", it is 7'2"), weighs more than I do (I weigh 200, it weighs I don't know how much more), can see much further than I can. I'm glad it is as wide as it is (42") & that it can accommodate, not counting the top board, 21 linear feet of material.

v.

Its poetry is its 4th dimension. I like to think that it is memorizing itself, its own contents.

vi.

The Green Bookcase is one of two personal possessions I would find it hardest to lose, so imbued is it with memory, faith, meaning.

vii.

I'm glad that it's built strong, that its boards have not warped & probably won't.

viii.

The Green Bookcase came into being & was found by
someone who never played a video game, or worked with
a digital camera, or had a cell-phone (though he plans
to get one), or sent a text-message. He did move from
manual typewriter to electric typewriter to computer word-
processing & e-mail (thanks to a son versed in techno-
things), but all of his writing is first done in cursive. He
doesn't have a blog or a web-site. He harbors no hard & fast
feelings against gizmo breakthroughs, would even like to be
hip & adept with one of these hand-held combinations that
are phones/TVs/libraries/music halls/photography studios/
cyber arboretums & zoos/ global positioning systems/ garage
door openers & who knows what else, & he could afford one,
but hasn't wanted to take time to learn to be proficient
with one. He's lived a life with family & friends, with
nature, with students, with hard-copy books. Tom Bissell

has written about how all
generations of writers have had
their distractions. He's wary
of but not in despair about
machine-generated contemporary
entertainment obsessions.
Bissell does say, however,
"Every literary person, then, is
a conservationist in the fight
for increasingly endangered
consciousness." How much of your
own consciousness, or mine, is
pixel, how much plankton?

ix.

Some poems, some works of art exhibit rhythmic
velocity. This one does not.

The Green Bookcase exists in a slow flow of littlemag
time, like snow falling through snow.

x.

The magazines may be thought of as the primary medium
of this work. At the same time, *The Green Bookcase* maybe
thought of as an homage to these magazines.

xi.

Some years ago I heard about, but did not see, an exhibition of artists' palettes. I liked the whole concept, as a revelation of personality, technique, tendency. Now,

The Green Bookcase has become the palette for this prose piece. Or is it, at least sometimes, the other way around? My mind, as I think about this object, is a palette knife.

WILLIAM HEYEN:

Lists and Things

1.

What is left in a northern garden
on New Year's Day
is a shadow of its summer. Gone
with the cold rain
yesterday
the snow left its dirty frost
to surround a sunflower's scrannel
stalk that lost
its sunburst
head at the last
harvest. I remember that it fell
spitting a few dry seeds
in early September,
leaving its green foot
to stand in autumn weeds
and winter weather.

2.

The dead watermelon
and pumpkin
patches
are tangles of brown and withered vines,
where,
nder broad leaves
any a toad

xii.

In the preface to my one book of stories, *The Hummingbird Corporation*, I say that I hope these fictions will keep my other writings company, that my poems will now be less lonely than they would otherwise be. I hope that now *The Green Bookcase* will in the same way keep my books & my now-being-published (slowly) 50-year ongoing journal company, that they will all converse with & help

to integrate/complicate/expand/ensoul one another.
This work of art is part of my bibliography.

xiii.

I've probably written about little magazines dozens
of times in my journal. Just now, taking down a volume &
reading at random, I spotted this paragraph from 12/5/90:
"Bill Tremblay took 'The Scar' & 'By the Time I Loved Him'
for *Colorado Review*. I've said now & then that my love
affair with little magazines is over, but these past several
months, thinking of how hungry I was back in my early
years, & with the luck of writing good new poems & having
acceptances from *APR*, *Georgia Review*, *Ploughshares* & others,
remembering walking to graduate classes at Ohio University
while thinking of submissions & many rejections & then once
in a while an acceptance, I feel a low flame again. All those
labors of love out there to receive mine."

xiv.

Many of my writings in these magazines did not make
it into any of my books & will not be published again, but
these writings—the earliest magazine here is from 1962—peep,
like chicks, glad to have been born. They've no ambition—
some are blind in one or both eyes, some misshapen—but just
keep peeping & scratching in straw. They have no future
other than to be here, & to welcome visitors.

xv.

I'm glad *The Green Bookcase* has an aspect of
contemplation, of repose, even while it holds, as poetry
does, all our contraries.

xvi.

Its tone: maybe romantic-elegiac, with a tinge of the obsessive-heroic.

xvii.

It's a flowing gloom this 4 a.m., a slow wind in bushes & trees. I'm inside in my easy chair, couldn't sleep much, but it's a pleasure to be up early, following the ink flow of this sentence, this paragraph. A few fireflies are still winking their phosphor locations. They remind me that a magazine called *Firefly* is part of *The Green Bookcase*. Offhand, I don't remember its year or what poem or poems of mine strobe from within that magazine, but for just a moment, now, out in the shed & out of sight, *The Green Bookcase* seems to me a gathering place of fireflies. I can almost see it through two walls, & will now go to it to make sure that it is still there.

xviii.

I'm glad that the shelf edges were run through a shaper. As a boy in Nesconset on Long Island I watched my father grind pairs of shaping blades, tighten them into his machine's bit, & then run boards through to create moldings. I'm very aware of the process that gave five boards here their soft-rhyming edges.

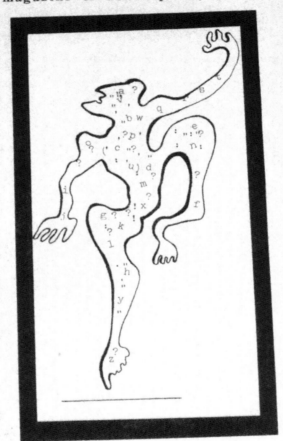

WILLIWAW

magazine of contemporary poetry

Vol. 1, No. 1   Autumn 1987

xix.

Little magazines, so disposable—but someone was not disposed, in this case, to dispose of them. Walt said that maybe the grass was the flag of his disposition, "out of hopeful green stuff woven." I guess this bookcase is the flag of my disposition.

xx.

One summer day I was sitting in front of the magazines when I noticed a small translucent spider spinning down from a shelf edge. I thought of course of Walt's "Noiseless Patient Spider" that sends filament, filament, filament out of itself, hoping to connect across the vast distances by way of faith. The poet imagines this spider as his soul. I'm thinking now of a spider spinning down through this prose piece, attached to the title, unreeling itself through the years.

xxi.

Nothing sensational or shocking or overtly symbolic here, no extreme aesthetic behavior, no wings mounted on its sides. It is not painted with flames as though it represented the library destroyed at Alexandria. It has not been invented, but created almost accidentally, almost unconsciously, & discovered. *The Green Bookcase* may hold at least one magazine from each of our fifty states, but it is not emblazoned with stars & stripes & called "America."

The China Bull

I

As if hating its fragilities intact
...d bull glares from a china cup,
...t to stamp ceramic

xxii.

I realize that I've been indulging myself in pathetic fallacies here, but to what extent may it be said that an object possesses mind? If I am quiet before this one, it seems to be thinking, or in REM sleep.

xxiii.

The intersection, the fusion of literature & the fine arts.

xxiv.

I dreamed that during one of our wrong wars our president died. He'd given a speech in front of a large auditorium audience, & then had suffered a stroke or heart attack. Secret service men carried him from that place on a stretcher that was *The Green Bookcase*.

xxv.

I think that *The Green Bookcase* does not think of itself as either window or door. I think it thinks of itself at night as a tree, an evergreen, & during the day as a daydream.

xxvi.
Being of such bohemian nature, made of such common materials & being of such quiet presence & import, this work of art is not likely to be stolen or defaced by a madman with hammer or blowtorch. Or, in another century, will it be, for just those reasons?

xxvii.
Peep.

xxviii.

My contributions to all these magazines speak of times when I was in flux, uncertainty (as, in fact, I still am). Even writings that eventually made their ways into my books were revised (& some will be revised again). There is always, as Joyce Carol Oates has said, "Another project that has been begun, another concatenation of indefinable states." As *The Green Bookcase* changes over time—for it will change even when dusted or when someone takes down a magazine & then replaces it—it acknowledges the flux & creativity at the heart of impermanence.

JOSEPH BRUCHAC RUTH STONE KRISTINE RUSCH

ROSEBUD®

The Magazine For People Who Enjoy Good Writing

ISSUE 34

CAN 11.95 / USA 7.95

xxix.

I've just noticed that each shelf holds about a decade
of my contributions to magazines. *The Green Bookcase* grows
to my ground in time & Time something like this:

Top shelf: 1960s
2nd shelf: 1970s & The Turtle Review
3rd shelf: 1980s
4th shelf: 1990s
5th shelf: 2000s
6th shelf: 2000s & clock

xxx.

This piece of prose, this essay you're reading, *The Green Bookcase:* a poet-friend who read an early draft of it, Roy Bentley, suggested that it might be the basis for a play, the two brothers—one the living retired professor-poet & one the cop-woodworker in his after-dimension—discussing the object. In the end, there might it be, in its shed, alone at night, glowing softly, itself the answer to all the questions put to it. For such a play, should the clock's battery be replaced?

xxxi.

Maybe at some point a third character enters the stage. Yes, it's the brothers' high school coach, an Iwo Jima vet. He says, "What's all this chickenshit crap about a bookcase?" [*Grabs his crotch.*] "I got your bookcase hanging."

xxxii.

By the way, since, to begin with, *The Green Bookcase* itself & this prose piece are so self-reflexive, so self-referential, I've placed in one of the maroon boxes, too, the many drafts of these ruminations. By the way, early drafts mention the second possession I'd find it hardest to lose.

xxxiii.

Notice that I've not centered the three-word title of this prose piece above the text, but have placed it in upper-left position to correspond with the three file boxes. (I'd like to have this title printed in maroon, though one of its words is green. This goes back to the contraries I mentioned.)[See frontispiece and title page.]

xxxiv.

Each of these afterthoughts is a magazine. This one is called Afterthought.

xxxv.

I have treasured out my life in magazines.

xxxvi.

Speaking of T.S. Eliot, I don't have/*The Green Bookcase* doesn't have a copy of the Autumn 1967 *Shenandoah* which contains my review of young Tom's juvenilia, *Poems Written in Early Youth*, poems written between his 16th & 22nd birthdays. (I have the review itself in my book *Titanic & Iceberg: Early Essays & Reviews* [2006]—I worked from a xerox copy for this book, & don't know what happened to my copy or copies of that issue of *Shenandoah*, but *The Green Bookcase* will keep

its cyclopean eye open for one. Any chance that you have one?)

Wallace Stevens once noted that "some of one's early things give one the creeps." No doubt the old possum felt this way, too. Take for example this stanza from "A Fable for Feasters," which appeared in *Smith Academy Record* (1905). This was his first published poem. The student poet is versifying about a group of feasting monks:

They were possessors of rich lands and wide,
      An orchard, and a vineyard, and a dairy;
Whenever some old villainous baron died,
      He added to their hoards—a deed which ne'er he
Had done before—their fortune multiplied,
      As if they had been kept by a kind fairy.
      Alas! no fairy visited their host,
      Oh, no; much worse than that, they had a ghost.

Poem & book are filled with rhyme-stretching, inversion, artificial diction, & everything else about which the Imagists would become apoplectic. But usually, in poetry, ontology recapitulates phylogeny, most aspirers evolve through the same stages, & I can surely top Tom for beginning badness…. Let me find a stanza…. Yes, here's one from a magazine *The Green Bookcase* does harbor, *Approach 58* (1966). It's the third stanza of a poem called "Lists and Things" about a northern garden on New Year's Day when it is all muck & withered plants:

Two kinds of cabbage leaves
lie frozen
as if they shared
a private joke
with the slanted sun,
one, planted red,
still reddish. I wanted
to yank them, root,
heart, leaves
and all, but a gardener
anticipates still yet another
year, and dead things fertilize,
so I played wise.
My agrarian nature spoke
and I left their leaves and roots
to rot.

At the time, at least, as bad as this is, I did seem to anticipate *The Green Bookcase* as a compost heap for whatever books of mine would, come other springs, grow from it. Though the jacket of my first book, *Depth of Field* (I'll put, self-referentially again, a still shrink-wrapped copy in one of the maroon boxes), which was published in 1970, was green—even my face on the back cover was green—"Lists and Things" was not one of its fifty-three poems. But here it is, still, among other garden scraps but among, too, poems that have managed to keep re-seeding themselves.

xxxvii.

I mentioned above that my other bookcases do not have the depth of character of this one. Cases filled with my chapbooks & books ("A" items) or anthologies ("B" items) seem too sure of themselves, do not have the disheveled charm or sense of evanescence & vulnerability & sheer fortitude of *The Green Bookcase* with its "C" items. *The Green Bookcase* is on the edge of non-being. It is a spell that might too easily, without forethought & fore-seeing, be broken; its life might any moment be translated, like a pickerel from Walden Pond, into "the thin air of heaven." One of my 2,000+ 13-syllable scherzi, "The Green Bookcase": "How can I hold it together / when I'm dead weather?" Or, "Heyen can't hold it together / when he's dead weather." Or, "Can Heyen hold it together / when he's dead weather?"

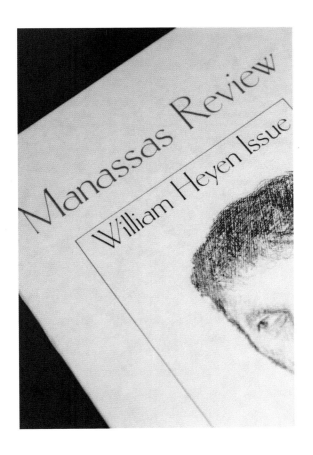

xxxviii.

Jim Harrison in his memoir *Off to the Side* says that "Perhaps the singular reason young poets are attracted to writing programs is out of loneliness, the need to be in the company of their own strange kind." We could take this idea in several directions, but I'll for now take it off to the side this way: maybe *The Green Bookcase* is a writing program; certainly, literary mags are a strange kind, now less lonely & scattered than they otherwise would have been except for this sympathetic home, one that you might, by appreciating *The Green Bookcase*, make secure for them.

xxxix.

I've not printed up & placed in the bookcase my
contributions to online zines. I'm content to let these be
in their electrical ether, even if I sense that they are
lonely for body. I've not included, either, magazines with
reviews of my books. Unless I've also contributed to these
issues, I've not saved them.

xl.

Maybe what led to my sudden recognition of what was in
my shed was that green has been in my mind. In my upcoming
book-length poem *To William Merwin*, I mention Walt's grass,
Thoreau's green-painted desk in his Walden cabin, a green
felt-covered table in Independence Hall in Philadelphia on
which I saw Ben Franklin's eyeglasses, Theodore Roethke's
greenhouse poems, sprigs of cedar in holiday cards sent
from Oregon to our family by William & Dorothy Stafford,
the gangrene of a moray eel bite, the greening voice of
Dylan Thomas; & my poem ends while thinking of Merwin's
translation of *Sir Gawain & the Green Knight*.

xli.

For every acceptance from a magazine over the years,
I've been rejected several times. If *The Green Bookcase* is
a song of acceptance, & it is, it is still hard for me to
hear it.

xlii.

By now I feel
that you & I and
this ensemble—
including the chair
& this prose piece—
have grown together.
I've been grateful
for your patience
as you've begun to
find me as I've begun
to sound *The Green
Bookcase*.

xliii.

It is completely
by chance that the
single metal bookend
that I've used to
hold up the most
recent magazines is
green. Not.

xliv.

Speaking of green, if some person or gallery buys this
sui-generis piece from me, I'll have been paid for all the
poems that magazines did not pay for except in the copies
that became part of this work. If I do sell it or otherwise
place it somewhere, I hope I'll be able to visit it from
time to time, add to it, peer into it in ramifying ways. If
I sell it to you, say on eBay, by the way, you'll have to
pick it up. (I wonder what starting bid I should set, &,
if there's a reserve price, how much this should be. Some
of these mags are worth 5, 10, 20+ bucks—an early *Wormwood
Review*, e.g., with Charles Bukowski in it; an early *Ball
State University Forum* with a Raymond Carver story—but
is the whole worth more than the sum of its parts? Money
isn't the point, but, as James Dickey said to me, "the more
they pay, the harder they listen.") If a gallery paid for
it, or at least accepted it into its so-called permanent
collection, *The Green Bookcase*, excepting the attack of
terrorists or an apocalypse, would not find itself at the
curb…. In the end, as I write this, I don't know what will
happen to this work of art, but it does seem to have come
to calm selfhood so that it does not rely on a particular
context: it will continue to embody & exude meanings
whether it stands in a penthouse apartment somewhere, or
art gallery, or barn. But I hope it will not be misread
& dismembered, hope that someone will always become the
advocate for it that I have almost accidentally but now of
necessity have come to be.

xlv.

　　Afternote after afternote here I've wanted to say something about the plastic bags, but what? I don't think the magazines have suffered from being inside these ubiquitous & environmentally problematic protectors. They are certainly a part of the texture of the whole. Feel free to open & close & retape them as you see fit. Without them, the bookcase's voice would have been hoarse, its tongues diseased (singular voice, plural tongues). (Note to the succession of curators: feel free to keep or remove some or all of these plastic bags as you see fit.)

me II ⚓ 3/4   Autumn 84/Spring

BLUEFISH

Appleman, Rae Armantrout, Bill Berks
ames Bertolino, Christopher Buckley,
Butscher, Hans Carossa, Vince Cleme
Deguy, Sharon Doubiago, Larry Eigr
lliot, Theodore Enslin, Clayton Eshler

xlvi.

I said above that I've arranged the mags chronologically. I said this thoughtlessly without remembering that, yes, they were at least shelved year by year, but I haven't paid attention to seasons & have often arranged the mags by size & color toward an overall effect/ countenance. (& why not, chronology being tenuous in the first place, a poem in a 2004 magazine maybe having been written in 2001, e.g.? & why not, *The Green Bookcase* being a complex of circuitous temporal entanglements & wormholes?)

xlvii.

As I write this particular paragraph—by the way, these afterthoughts are not chronological—my wife & I are celebrating our 45th anniversary (July 7, 2007). As I write, *The Green Bookcase* stands ready to receive new issues of magazines that have accepted me: *Kestrel, The Kenyon Review, Ontario Review, Redactions, Review Revue, Margie, Poetry Kanto* (Japan), & two issues each of *Great River Review, The Seventh Quarry* (Wales), & *The Southern Review*. Let me be silly: every time *The Green Bookcase* receives a new magazine, it renews its wedding vows.

xlviii.

Richard Wilbur once said that he knew he was done with a poem when he felt he'd exhausted his present sense of the subject. Over as much time in Time that I have left, this work of art will be exhausting my own present sense of the subject, & then will go on, more competently, on its own until whenever. & now in this prose piece—silliness being one sign—I've almost exhausted my present sense of the subject.

xlix.

Notice that the magazines of the later decades become more spine-colorful. I think that this is to compensate me as I grow grayer.

1.

Do you notice the abrasion on the front of the third file box? I've watercolored it in a little.

li.

Yesterday (10/17/07), while I was making a few last brush-strokes here, my book-length poem *To William Merwin* arrived in the mail, its cover dominated by Diamond Head rendered in shades of green by artist Harvey A. Warren in 1964. I'll place a copy of this book next to *Depth of Field*. Notice how the mauve-maroon above Diamond Head suggests the maroon file boxes atop the bookcase. Consider how, were you ever to read them, *Depth of Field* (1970) & *To William Merwin* (2007), the only two "A" items in this ensemble, enclose, make circular this work of art.

lii.

Yesterday (March 19, 2008) I learned that *Ontario Review*, after the death of its editor Raymond Smith, will cease publication this spring after thirty-four years. I had poems in its first issue, & then in about fifteen other issues—all here in *The Green Bookcase*—and Ray had accepted poems for a future number. *Ontario Review* is dead. Long live, here & elsewhere, *Ontario Review*.

liii.

Just two more peeps, the story & poem I mentioned. When I was sixteen & beginning college I developed acute feelings of inferiority. Although in time I earned decent grades & became an all-American athlete, I still held my hand over my face & had to struggle just to order from a

waitress at a diner. These often debilitating feelings hung on even into a strong marriage & fatherhood. The routine dismissal of my writing by the editors of magazines certainly did not help solve my self-esteem issues (I like the way the word *issues* works here now), but was manageable. I'd get a rejection, but usually had other submissions in the mail, & had hope for the next batch of poems. But one graduate school year I returned to Athens, Ohio, with my family from weeks of Christmas break at my in-laws' farmhouse in Nashville, New York, outside Forestville. In my mailbox were 8-10 manila envelopes, each one a rejection.

   To say the least, I was glum for weeks, for months. It had been hard for us even to afford the postage, but the main thing was that I was not being assured that I was of any worth, that the work I was sending out was actually poetry, that my guilt-ridden all-night writing sessions with cigarettes & coffee were anything more than vain striving & delusion & time taken from family & from more practical studies. But one day the following summer, back

in Nashville, I went to the mailbox—I can still see me on that country road under the century-old maples—& tore open an envelope to read that *The Southern Review* had accepted a poem of mine. Imagine that, the perfect-bound & handsome venerable & prestigious *The Southern Review*, founded in 1935 by Robert Penn Warren & others, had accepted my poem "The China Bull." In later years, as evidenced by *The Green Bookcase*, I'd appear in this magazine fairly often, but I will always be grateful for this memorable acceptance from readers far away who even paid me for my poem. *The Green Bookcase*, as it enters Time, manifests such encouragement from so many.

CHAUTAUQUA
LITERARY JOURNAL

CHauTauQua
ISSUE 6

The Green Bookcase, as it enters Time, manifests such encouragement from so many. At Ohio University, I'd eventually walk up the hill from married student housing to classes in Ellis Hall while repeating to myself a comforting & consoling mantra that I can still hear—"*The Southern Review, The Wormwood Review, Western Humanities Review, The Writer's Voice, Prairie Schooner*"—as I gained in confidence & as *The Green Bookcase* began to come into being.

liv.

Book Store, 2045

It's okay now, close down, I'm here
        in your city's dark. It's okay, I'm here, my poems
in The Southern Review where magazines crowd
        the furthest lowest shelf.

Your city exists these years within a fuchsia haze,
        mass catastrophes just past &/or soon-to-come—
such stores as yours anomaly, but there are still a few,
        within & across my vision. It's okay,

whether you're the manager or the last customer,
        so shut the door, step up & out into West 47th,
get to your train, if it's still running,
        get to your own family, whatever else you do,

any way you can. I'm content to exist here while gotham
        seems to disappear except for the glow
from a surge protector feeding the live oak logo
        on the spine of my memorial home.

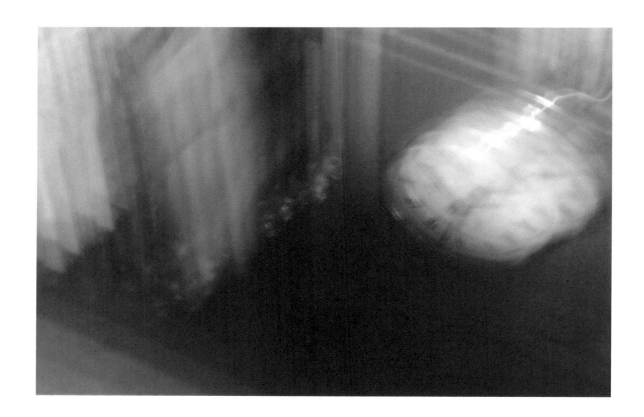

Afterword, 2018

{ There I was, leaving a NYC bookstore (the Gotham in my mind) for an apocalyptic future of some kind, ending my elegiac & eccentric essay with a poem wherein I console myself because somewhere, somewhere, somewhere my name & my poem (& at least a suggestion of my having existed, a suggestion of my being) will exist, somewhere, in some dimension. Years later, now, as Karla Linn Merrifield completes a second edition of *The Green Bookcase*, my view of the human future still fearful at best, I still console myself that somewhere, somewhere, whatever happens, I will have left at least a poem in a magazine on some bottom shelf somewhere, even if there will be no one there to read me. (Please see Samuel Bak's painting on the cover of my book *The Candle*, his "The Art of Reading.") It sounds to me now, years later, that a resigned romantic speaks my poem. Thoreau said that above all else he didn't want to practice resignation. Maybe the existence of my poem, & of this book, & of the writing we all do, is evidence still not of total resignation but of action & commitment, of love? At the end of *The Sun Also Rises* Jake asks Brett, "Isn't it pretty to think so?" }

~~~

…somewhere,

somewhere,

whatever happens,

I will have left at

least a poem in

a magazine on

some bottom shelf

somewhere, even

if there will be

no one there

to read me.

~~~

~~~

The Green Bookcase is now housed at
Kenneth Kelbaugh's Before Your Quiet
Eyes bookstore in Rochester, NY.

~~~

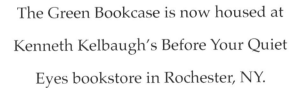

IS HEYEN SPEAKING

By Philip Brady

absorbing webs"
tissue to the dea
Some might
Tram on the groi
nal Mooney, I ru
I stretch beyond
"This is Heyen sp
Steve Oristaglio (
bankers, Ezra), be
mind, amotic

WLLIAM HEYEN is Professor of English/Poet-in Residence Emeritus at The College at Brockport, his undergraduate alma mater. His graduate degrees are from Ohio University. A former Senior Fulbright Lecturer in American Literature in Germany, he has won NEA, Guggenheim, American Academy & Institute of Arts & Letters, and other fellowships and awards. He is the editor of several books, including September 11, 2001: American Writers Respond, and the author of more than thirty books, including Noise in the Trees, an American Library Association Notable Book; Crazy Horse in Stillness, winner of the Small Press Book Award; Shoah Train: Poems, a Finalist for the 2004 National Book Award; and A Poetics of Hiroshima, a Chautauqua Literary & Scientific Circle (CLSC) selection in 2010. Other recent books include Straight's Suite for Craig Cotter & Frank O'Hara, The Football Corporations, and Hiroshima Suite. In 2016, Etruscan Press published his The Candle: Poems of Our Twentieth Century Holocausts, a CLSC main selection. Volumes of his extensive journal are appearing from time to time with H_NGM_N Books. In 2011, Heyen was awarded an Honorary Doctorate of Humane Letters from SUNY.

KARLA LINN MERRIFIELD, who studied creative writing under William Heyen, has thirteen books to her credit, the newest of which is *Psyche's Scroll*, a book-length poem, published by The Poetry Box Select in June 2018. Her *Godwit: Poems of Canada* (FootHills Publishing) received the 2009 Eiseman Award for Poetry. Merrifield's photography has appeared in Outdoor, Sea Stories, *The Centrifugal Eye*, and *Biblioteka Alexandria*, among many magazines and journals. In 2009, High Falls Gallery in Rochester, NY, featured her avian photography in a one-woman show, *Dawn of Migration and Other Audubon Dreams*, and the Everglades National Park Coe Visitor Center presented a dozen of her photographs in its 2011 exhibition of works by the park's artists-in-residence. She is assistant editor and poetry book reviewer for *The Centrifugal Eye*. Visit her blog, *Vagabond Poet Redux* at http://karlainn.blogspot.com. (Photo by Ken Kelbaugh)

Hollybrook House Press